•VEHICLE DETAILS•

CW00517635

REGISTRATION	
MAKE	
MODEL	
COLOR	
DATE PURCHASED	
MILEAGE	

INSURANCE DETAILS	
EMERGENCY CONTACT	

VEHICLE INSURANCE DETAILS

INSURANCE COMPANY	START DATE	END DATE	POLICY NUMBER	COST	NO CLAIMS YEARS	CLAIM NUMBER	BREAKDOWN RECOVERY DETAILS

VEHICLE INSURANCE DETAILS

INSURANCE COMPANY	START DATE	END DATE	POLICY NUMBER	COST	NO CLAIMS YEARS	CLAIM NUMBER	BREAKDOWN RECOVERY DETAILS

VEHICLE INSURANCE DETAILS

INSURANCE COMPANY	START DATE	END DATE	POLICY NUMBER	COST	NO CLAIMS YEARS	CLAIM NUMBER	BREAKDOWN RECOVERY DETAILS

VEHICLE INSURANCE DETAILS

INSURANCE COMPANY	START DATE	END DATE	POLICY NUMBER	COST	NO CLAIMS YEARS	CLAIM NUMBER	BREAKDOWN RECOVERY DETAILS

VEHICLE INSURANCE DETAILS

INSURANCE COMPANY	START DATE	END DATE	POLICY NUMBER	COST	NO CLAIMS YEARS	CLAIM NUMBER	BREAKDOWN RECOVERY DETAILS

VEHICLE INSURANCE DETAILS

INSURANCE COMPANY	START DATE	END DATE	POLICY NUMBER	COST	NO CLAIMS YEARS	CLAIM NUMBER	BREAKDOWN RECOVERY DETAILS

VEHICLE INSURANCE DETAILS

INSURANCE COMPANY	START DATE	END DATE	POLICY NUMBER	COST	NO CLAIMS YEARS	CLAIM NUMBER	BREAKDOWN RECOVERY DETAILS

VEHICLE INSURANCE DETAILS

INSURANCE COMPANY	START DATE	END DATE	POLICY NUMBER	COST	NO CLAIMS YEARS	CLAIM NUMBER	BREAKDOWN RECOVERY DETAILS

VEHICLE REGISTRATION LOG

VEHICLE	ENGINE SIZE	START DATE	END DATE	COST

VEHICLE REGISTRATION LOG

VEHICLE	ENGINE SIZE	START DATE	END DATE	COST

VEHICLE REGISTRATION LOG

VEHICLE	ENGINE SIZE	START DATE	END DATE	COST

VEHICLE REGISTRATION LOG

VEHICLE	ENGINE SIZE	START DATE	END DATE	COST

VEHICLE REGISTRATION LOG

VEHICLE	ENGINE SIZE	START DATE	END DATE	COST

VEHICLE REGISTRATION LOG

VEHICLE	ENGINE SIZE	START DATE	END DATE	COST

VEHICLE REGISTRATION LOG

VEHICLE	ENGINE SIZE	START DATE	END DATE	COST

VEHICLE REGISTRATION LOG

VEHICLE	ENGINE SIZE	START DATE	END DATE	COST

MOT/ INSPECTION LOG

GARAGE DETAILS:

DATE:

CAR DETAILS

REPAIRS/ISSUES?
_____
_____
_____
_____
_____
_____

START DATE

_____

END DATE

GARAGE STAMP

MAINTENANCE/ SERVICE RECORD

DATE	MILEAGE	TYRES REPLACED	WHEEL ALIGNMENT	BALANCE TYRES	AIR FILTERS CHANGED	OIL CHANGED	BRAKE FLUID	SPARK PLUGS	FUEL FILTER	TRANSMISSSION	BATTERIES	WIPER BLADES	RADIATOR	OTHER	OTHER

NOTES

_____

_____

_____

_____

_____

_____

MOT/ INSPECTION LOG

GARAGE DETAILS:

DATE:

CAR DETAILS

REPAIRS/ISSUES?
_____
_____
_____
_____
_____
_____

START DATE

_____

END DATE

GARAGE STAMP

MAINTENANCE/ SERVICE RECORD

DATE	MILEAGE	TYRES REPLACED	WHEEL ALIGNMENT	BALANCE TYRES	AIR FLITERS CHANGED	OIL CHANGED	BRAKE FLUID	SPARK PLUGS	FUEL FILTER	TRANSMISSSION	BATTERIES	WIPER BLADES	RADIATOR	OTHER	OTHER

NOTES

_____

_____

_____

_____

_____

MOT/ INSPECTION LOG

GARAGE DETAILS:

DATE:

CAR DETAILS

REPAIRS/ISSUES?

START DATE

_____

END DATE

GARAGE STAMP

MAINTENANCE/ SERVICE RECORD

DATE	MILEAGE	TYRES REPLACED	WHEEL ALIGNMENT	BALANCE TYRES	AIR FLITERS CHANGED	OIL CHANGED	BRAKE FLUID	SPARK PLUGS	FUEL FILTER	TRANSMISSSION	BATTERIES	WIPER BLADES	RADIATOR	OTHER	OTHER

NOTES

_____

_____

_____

_____

_____

MOT/ INSPECTION LOG

GARAGE DETAILS:

DATE:

CAR DETAILS

REPAIRS/ISSUES?

START DATE

_____

END DATE

GARAGE STAMP

MAINTENANCE/ SERVICE RECORD

DATE	MILEAGE	TYRES REPLACED	WHEEL ALIGNMENT	BALANCE TYRES	AIR FILTERS CHANGED	OIL CHANGED	BRAKE FLUID	SPARK PLUGS	FUEL FILTER	TRANSMISSSION	BATTERIES	WIPER BLADES	RADIATOR	OTHER	OTHER

NOTES

_____

_____

_____

_____

_____

MOT/ INSPECTION LOG

GARAGE DETAILS:

DATE:

START DATE

_____

END DATE

CAR DETAILS

GARAGE STAMP

REPAIRS/ISSUES? _____
_____
_____
_____
_____
_____

MAINTENANCE/ SERVICE RECORD

DATE	MILEAGE	TYRES REPLACED	WHEEL ALIGNMENT	BALANCE TYRES	AIR FLITERS CHANGED	OIL CHANGED	BRAKE FLUID	SPARK PLUGS	FUEL FILTER	TRANSMISSSION	BATTERIES	WIPER BLADES	RADIATOR	OTHER	OTHER

NOTES

_____

_____

_____

_____

_____

_____

MOT/ INSPECTION LOG

GARAGE DETAILS:

DATE:

CAR DETAILS

REPAIRS/ISSUES?
_____
_____
_____
_____
_____
_____

START DATE

_____

END DATE

GARAGE STAMP

MAINTENANCE/ SERVICE RECORD

DATE	MILEAGE	TYRES REPLACED	WHEEL ALIGNMENT	BALANCE TYRES	AIR FLITERS CHANGED	OIL CHANGED	BRAKE FLUID	SPARK PLUGS	FUEL FILTER	TRANSMISSSION	BATTERIES	WIPER BLADES	RADIATOR	OTHER	OTHER

NOTES

_____

_____

_____

_____

_____

MOT/ INSPECTION LOG

GARAGE DETAILS:

DATE:

CAR DETAILS

REPAIRS/ISSUES?

_____
_____
_____
_____
_____
_____

START DATE

_____

END DATE

GARAGE STAMP

MAINTENANCE/ SERVICE RECORD

DATE	MILEAGE	TYRES REPLACED	WHEEL ALIGNMENT	BALANCE TYRES	AIR FLITERS CHANGED	OIL CHANGED	BRAKE FLUID	SPARK PLUGS	FUEL FILTER	TRANSMISSSION	BATTERIES	WIPER BLADES	RADIATOR	OTHER	OTHER

NOTES

_____

_____

_____

_____

_____

_____

MOT/ INSPECTION LOG

GARAGE DETAILS:

DATE:

CAR DETAILS

REPAIRS/ISSUES?

START DATE

_____

END DATE

GARAGE STAMP

MAINTENANCE/ SERVICE RECORD

DATE	MILEAGE	TYRES REPLACED	WHEEL ALIGNMENT	BALANCE TYRES	AIR FLITERS CHANGED	OIL CHANGED	BRAKE FLUID	SPARK PLUGS	FUEL FILTER	TRANSMISSSION	BATTERIES	WIPER BLADES	RADIATOR	OTHER	OTHER

NOTES

_____

_____

_____

_____

_____

MOT/ INSPECTION LOG

GARAGE DETAILS:

DATE:

CAR DETAILS

REPAIRS/ISSUES?
_____
_____
_____
_____
_____
_____

START DATE

_____

END DATE

GARAGE STAMP

MAINTENANCE/ SERVICE RECORD

DATE	MILEAGE	TYRES REPLACED	WHEEL ALIGNMENT	BALANCE TYRES	AIR FLITERS CHANGED	OIL CHANGED	BRAKE FLUID	SPARK PLUGS	FUEL FILTER	TRANSMISSSION	BATTERIES	WIPER BLADES	RADIATOR	OTHER	OTHER

NOTES

_____

_____

_____

_____

_____

MOT/ INSPECTION LOG

GARAGE DETAILS:

DATE:

CAR DETAILS

REPAIRS/ISSUES?

START DATE

_____

END DATE

GARAGE STAMP

MAINTENANCE/ SERVICE RECORD

DATE	MILEAGE	TYRES REPLACED	WHEEL ALIGNMENT	BALANCE TYRES	AIR FLITERS CHANGED	OIL CHANGED	BRAKE FLUID	SPARK PLUGS	FUEL FILTER	TRANSMISSSION	BATTERIES	WIPER BLADES	RADIATOR	OTHER	OTHER

NOTES

_____

_____

_____

_____

_____

MOT/ INSPECTION LOG

GARAGE DETAILS:

DATE:

START DATE

_____

END DATE

CAR DETAILS

REPAIRS/ISSUES?

GARAGE STAMP

MAINTENANCE/ SERVICE RECORD

DATE	MILEAGE	TYRES REPLACED	WHEEL ALIGNMENT	BALANCE TYRES	AIR FLITERS CHANGED	OIL CHANGED	BRAKE FLUID	SPARK PLUGS	FUEL FILTER	TRANSMISSSION	BATTERIES	WIPER BLADES	RADIATOR	OTHER	OTHER

NOTES

MOT/ INSPECTION LOG

GARAGE DETAILS:

DATE:

CAR DETAILS

REPAIRS/ISSUES?

_____

_____

_____

_____

_____

_____

START DATE

_____

END DATE

GARAGE STAMP

MAINTENANCE/ SERVICE RECORD

DATE	MILEAGE	TYRES REPLACED	WHEEL ALIGNMENT	BALANCE TYRES	AIR FILTERS CHANGED	OIL CHANGED	BRAKE FLUID	SPARK PLUGS	FUEL FILTER	TRANSMISSSION	BATTERIES	WIPER BLADES	RADIATOR	OTHER	OTHER

NOTES

_____

_____

_____

_____

_____

MOT/ INSPECTION LOG

GARAGE DETAILS:

DATE:

CAR DETAILS

REPAIRS/ISSUES?
_____
_____
_____
_____
_____
_____

START DATE

_____

END DATE

GARAGE STAMP

MAINTENANCE/ SERVICE RECORD

DATE	MILEAGE	TYRES REPLACED	WHEEL ALIGNMENT	BALANCE TYRES	AIR FILTERS CHANGED	OIL CHANGED	BRAKE FLUID	SPARK PLUGS	FUEL FILTER	TRANSMISSION	BATTERIES	WIPER BLADES	RADIATOR	OTHER	OTHER

NOTES

_____

_____

_____

_____

_____

MOT/ INSPECTION LOG

GARAGE DETAILS:

DATE:

CAR DETAILS

REPAIRS/ISSUES?
_____
_____
_____
_____
_____
_____

START DATE

_____

END DATE

GARAGE STAMP

MAINTENANCE/ SERVICE RECORD

DATE	MILEAGE	TYRES REPLACED	WHEEL ALIGNMENT	BALANCE TYRES	AIR FILTERS CHANGED	OIL CHANGED	BRAKE FLUID	SPARK PLUGS	FUEL FILTER	TRANSMISSION	BATTERIES	WIPER BLADES	RADIATOR	OTHER	OTHER

NOTES

_____

_____

_____

_____

_____

MOT/ INSPECTION LOG

GARAGE DETAILS:

DATE:

CAR DETAILS

REPAIRS/ISSUES?

START DATE

_____

END DATE

GARAGE STAMP

MAINTENANCE/ SERVICE RECORD

DATE	MILEAGE	TYRES REPLACED	WHEEL ALIGNMENT	BALANCE TYRES	AIR FLITERS CHANGED	OIL CHANGED	BRAKE FLUID	SPARK PLUGS	FUEL FILTER	TRANSMISSSION	BATTERIES	WIPER BLADES	RADIATOR	OTHER	OTHER

NOTES

MOT/ INSPECTION LOG

GARAGE DETAILS:

DATE:

CAR DETAILS

REPAIRS/ISSUES?

START DATE

_____

END DATE

GARAGE STAMP

MAINTENANCE/ SERVICE RECORD

DATE	MILEAGE	TYRES REPLACED	WHEEL ALIGNMENT	BALANCE TYRES	AIR FILTERS CHANGED	OIL CHANGED	BRAKE FLUID	SPARK PLUGS	FUEL FILTER	TRANSMISSSION	BATTERIES	WIPER BLADES	RADIATOR	OTHER	OTHER

NOTES

_____

_____

_____

_____

_____

MOT/ INSPECTION LOG

GARAGE DETAILS:

DATE:

CAR DETAILS

REPAIRS/ISSUES?

START DATE

_____

END DATE

GARAGE STAMP

MAINTENANCE/ SERVICE RECORD

DATE	MILEAGE	TYRES REPLACED	WHEEL ALIGNMENT	BALANCE TYRES	AIR FLITERS CHANGED	OIL CHANGED	BRAKE FLUID	SPARK PLUGS	FUEL FILTER	TRANSMISSSION	BATTERIES	WIPER BLADES	RADIATOR	OTHER	OTHER

NOTES

_____
_____
_____
_____
_____

MOT/ INSPECTION LOG

GARAGE DETAILS:

DATE:

CAR DETAILS

REPAIRS/ISSUES?
_____
_____
_____
_____
_____
_____

START DATE

_____

END DATE

GARAGE STAMP

MAINTENANCE/ SERVICE RECORD

DATE	MILEAGE	TYRES REPLACED	WHEEL ALIGNMENT	BALANCE TYRES	AIR FLITERS CHANGED	OIL CHANGED	BRAKE FLUID	SPARK PLUGS	FUEL FILTER	TRANSMISSSION	BATTERIES	WIPER BLADES	RADIATOR	OTHER	OTHER

NOTES

MOT/ INSPECTION LOG

GARAGE DETAILS:

DATE:

CAR DETAILS

REPAIRS/ISSUES?

START DATE

_____

END DATE

GARAGE STAMP

MAINTENANCE/ SERVICE RECORD

DATE	MILEAGE	TYRES REPLACED	WHEEL ALIGNMENT	BALANCE TYRES	AIR FLITERS CHANGED	OIL CHANGED	BRAKE FLUID	SPARK PLUGS	FUEL FILTER	TRANSMISSSION	BATTERIES	WIPER BLADES	RADIATOR	OTHER	OTHER

NOTES

_____

_____

_____

_____

_____

MOT/ INSPECTION LOG

GARAGE DETAILS:

DATE:

CAR DETAILS

REPAIRS/ISSUES?
_____
_____
_____
_____
_____
_____

START DATE
_____

END DATE

GARAGE STAMP

MAINTENANCE/ SERVICE RECORD

DATE	MILEAGE	TYRES REPLACED	WHEEL ALIGNMENT	BALANCE TYRES	AIR FLITERS CHANGED	OIL CHANGED	BRAKE FLUID	SPARK PLUGS	FUEL FILTER	TRANSMISSSION	BATTERIES	WIPER BLADES	RADIATOR	OTHER	OTHER

NOTES

_____

_____

_____

_____

_____

MOT/ INSPECTION LOG

GARAGE DETAILS:

DATE:

CAR DETAILS

REPAIRS/ISSUES?
_____
_____
_____
_____
_____
_____

START DATE
_____

END DATE

GARAGE STAMP

MAINTENANCE/ SERVICE RECORD

DATE	MILEAGE	TYRES REPLACED	WHEEL ALIGNMENT	BALANCE TYRES	AIR FLITERS CHANGED	OIL CHANGED	BRAKE FLUID	SPARK PLUGS	FUEL FILTER	TRANSMISSSION	BATTERIES	WIPER BLADES	RADIATOR	OTHER	OTHER

NOTES

_____

_____

_____

_____

_____

MOT/ INSPECTION LOG

GARAGE DETAILS:

DATE:

CAR DETAILS

REPAIRS/ISSUES?

START DATE

_____

END DATE

GARAGE STAMP

MAINTENANCE/ SERVICE RECORD

DATE	MILEAGE	TYRES REPLACED	WHEEL ALIGNMENT	BALANCE TYRES	AIR FLITERS CHANGED	OIL CHANGED	BRAKE FLUID	SPARK PLUGS	FUEL FILTER	TRANSMISSSION	BATTERIES	WIPER BLADES	RADIATOR	OTHER	OTHER

NOTES

_____

_____

_____

_____

_____

MOT/ INSPECTION LOG

GARAGE DETAILS:

DATE:

CAR DETAILS

REPAIRS/ISSUES?
_____
_____
_____
_____
_____
_____

START DATE

_____

END DATE

GARAGE STAMP

MAINTENANCE/ SERVICE RECORD

DATE	MILEAGE	TYRES REPLACED	WHEEL ALIGNMENT	BALANCE TYRES	AIR FLITERS CHANGED	OIL CHANGED	BRAKE FLUID	SPARK PLUGS	FUEL FILTER	TRANSMISSSION	BATTERIES	WIPER BLADES	RADIATOR	OTHER	OTHER

NOTES

_____

_____

_____

_____

_____

MOT/ INSPECTION LOG

GARAGE DETAILS:

DATE:

CAR DETAILS

REPAIRS/ISSUES?
_____
_____
_____
_____
_____
_____

START DATE
_____

END DATE

GARAGE STAMP

MAINTENANCE/ SERVICE RECORD

DATE	MILEAGE	TYRES REPLACED	WHEEL ALIGNMENT	BALANCE TYRES	AIR FLITERS CHANGED	OIL CHANGED	BRAKE FLUID	SPARK PLUGS	FUEL FILTER	TRANSMISSSION	BATTERIES	WIPER BLADES	RADIATOR	OTHER	OTHER

NOTES

OTHER MAINTENANCE

DATE	VEHICLE	MILEAGE

GARAGE	COST
Item	
Item	
Item	
Item	
Item	
Item	
Item	
Item	

OTHER MAINTENANCE

DATE	VEHICLE	MILEAGE

GARAGE	COST
Item	
Item	
Item	
Item	
Item	
Item	
Item	
Item	

OTHER MAINTENANCE

DATE	VEHICLE	MILEAGE

GARAGE	COST
Item	
Item	
Item	
Item	
Item	
Item	
Item	
Item	

OTHER MAINTENANCE

DATE	VEHICLE	MILEAGE

GARAGE	COST
Item	
Item	
Item	
Item	
Item	
Item	
Item	
Item	

OTHER MAINTENANCE

DATE	VEHICLE	MILEAGE

GARAGE	
	COST
Item	
Item	
Item	
Item	
Item	
Item	
Item	
Item	

OTHER MAINTENANCE

DATE	VEHICLE	MILEAGE

GARAGE	COST
Item	
Item	
Item	
Item	
Item	
Item	
Item	
Item	

OTHER MAINTENANCE

DATE	VEHICLE	MILEAGE

GARAGE	COST
Item	
Item	
Item	
Item	
Item	
Item	
Item	
Item	

OTHER MAINTENANCE

DATE	VEHICLE	MILEAGE

GARAGE	COST
Item	
Item	
Item	
Item	
Item	
Item	
Item	
Item	

OTHER MAINTENANCE

DATE	VEHICLE	MILEAGE

GARAGE	COST
Item	
Item	
Item	
Item	
Item	
Item	
Item	
Item	

OTHER MAINTENANCE

DATE	VEHICLE	MILEAGE

GARAGE		
	COST	
Item		
Item		
Item		
Item		
Item		
Item		
Item		
Item		

OTHER MAINTENANCE

DATE	VEHICLE	MILEAGE	
GARAGE	**COST**		
Item			
Item			
Item			
Item			
Item			
Item			
Item			
Item			

OTHER MAINTENANCE

DATE	VEHICLE	MILEAGE

GARAGE		
	COST	
Item		
Item		
Item		
Item		
Item		
Item		
Item		
Item		

OTHER MAINTENANCE

DATE	VEHICLE	MILEAGE

GARAGE	COST
Item	
Item	
Item	
Item	
Item	
Item	
Item	
Item	

OTHER MAINTENANCE

DATE	VEHICLE	MILEAGE

GARAGE	COST
Item	
Item	
Item	
Item	
Item	
Item	
Item	
Item	

OTHER MAINTENANCE

DATE	VEHICLE	MILEAGE

GARAGE	
	COST
Item	
Item	
Item	
Item	
Item	
Item	
Item	
Item	

OTHER MAINTENANCE

DATE	VEHICLE	MILEAGE

GARAGE		
	COST	
Item		
Item		
Item		
Item		
Item		
Item		
Item		
Item		

GAS MILEAGE LOG

Month:

DATE	PRICE PER GALLON	GALLONS	TOTAL PRICE	START MILEAGE	END MILAGE	TOTAL MILAGE

GAS MILEAGE LOG

Month:

DATE	PRICE PER GALLON	GALLONS	TOTAL PRICE	START MILEAGE	END MILAGE	TOTAL MILAGE

GAS MILEAGE LOG

Month:

DATE	PRICE PER GALLON	GALLONS	TOTAL PRICE	START MILEAGE	END MILAGE	TOTAL MILAGE

GAS MILEAGE LOG

Month:

DATE	PRICE PER GALLON	GALLONS	TOTAL PRICE	START MILEAGE	END MILAGE	TOTAL MILAGE

GAS MILEAGE LOG

Month:

DATE	PRICE PER GALLON	GALLONS	TOTAL PRICE	START MILEAGE	END MILAGE	TOTAL MILAGE

GAS MILEAGE LOG

Month:

DATE	PRICE PER GALLON	GALLONS	TOTAL PRICE	START MILEAGE	END MILAGE	TOTAL MILAGE

GAS MILEAGE LOG

Month:

DATE	PRICE PER GALLON	GALLONS	TOTAL PRICE	START MILEAGE	END MILAGE	TOTAL MILAGE

GAS MILEAGE LOG

Month:

DATE	PRICE PER GALLON	GALLONS	TOTAL PRICE	START MILEAGE	END MILAGE	TOTAL MILAGE

GAS MILEAGE LOG

Month:

DATE	PRICE PER GALLON	GALLONS	TOTAL PRICE	START MILEAGE	END MILAGE	TOTAL MILAGE

GAS MILEAGE LOG

Month:

DATE	PRICE PER GALLON	GALLONS	TOTAL PRICE	START MILEAGE	END MILAGE	TOTAL MILAGE

NOTES

NOTES

NOTES

NOTES

NOTES

NOTES

NOTES

NOTES

NOTES